I0016535

App Inventor 2   Table of Contents – 2017 Edition

Learn tomorrow skills TODAY

with TomorrowSKILLS.COM

License Agreement

This book (the "Book") is a product provided by HobbyPRESS (being referred to as "HobbyPRESS" in this document), subject to your compliance with the terms and conditions set forth below. PLEASE READ THIS DOCUMENT CAREFULLY BEFORE ACCESSING OR USING THE BOOK. BY ACCESSING OR USING THE BOOK, YOU AGREE TO BE BOUND BY THE TERMS AND CONDITIONS SET FORTH BELOW. IF YOU DO NOT WISH TO BE BOUND BY THESE TERMS AND CONDITIONS, YOU MAY NOT ACCESS OR USE THE BOOK. HOBBYPRESS MAY MODIFY THIS AGREEMENT AT ANY TIME, AND SUCH MODIFICATIONS SHALL BE EFFECTIVE IMMEDIATELY UPON POSTING OF THE MODIFIED AGREEMENT ON THE CORPORATE SITE OF HOBBYPRESS. YOU AGREE TO REVIEW THE AGREEMENT PERIODICALLY TO BE AWARE OF SUCH MODIFICATIONS AND YOUR CONTINUED ACCESS OR USE OF THE BOOK SHALL BE DEEMED YOUR CONCLUSIVE ACCEPTANCE OF THE MODIFIED AGREEMENT.

Restrictions on Alteration

You may not modify the Book or create any derivative work of the Book or its accompanying documentation.   Derivative works include but are not limited to translations.

Restrictions on Copying

You may not copy any part of the Book unless formal written authorization is obtained from us.

Limitation of Liability

HobbyPRESS will not be held liable for any advice or suggestions given in this book. If the reader wants to follow a suggestion, it is at his or her own discretion. Suggestions are only offered to help.

IN NO EVENT WILL HOBBYPRESS BE LIABLE FOR (I) ANY INCIDENTAL, CONSEQUENTIAL, OR INDIRECT DAMAGES (INCLUDING, BUT NOT LIMITED TO, DAMAGES FOR LOSS OF PROFITS, BUSINESS INTERRUPTION, LOSS OF PROGRAMS OR INFORMATION, AND THE LIKE) ARISING OUT OF THE USE OF OR INABILITY TO USE THE BOOK. EVEN IF HOBBYPRESS OR ITS AUTHORIZED REPRESENTATIVES HAVE BEEN ADVISED OF THE POSSIBILITY OF SUCH DAMAGES, OR (II) ANY CLAIM ATTRIBUTABLE TO ERRORS, OMISSIONS, OR OTHER INACCURACIES IN THE BOOK. You agree to indemnify, defend and hold harmless HobbyPRESS, its officers, directors, employees, agents, licensors, suppliers and any third party information providers to the Book from and against all losses, expenses, damages and costs, including reasonable attorneys' fees, resulting from any violation of this Agreement (including negligent or wrongful conduct) by you or any other person using the Book.

Miscellaneous

This Agreement shall all be governed and construed in accordance with the laws of Hong Kong applicable to agreements made and to be performed in Hong Kong. You agree that any legal action or proceeding between HobbyPRESS and you for any purpose concerning this Agreement or the parties' obligations hereunder shall be brought exclusively in a court of competent jurisdiction sitting in Hong Kong.

About the TomorrowSKILLS Series

Give yourself a strong head start in computer programming with our TomorrowSKILLS books, which are published fresh in 2017. Through these books you will learn how programming works and how simple programs may be created using ready-made resources and modern drag-and-drop programming environments.

Basic Requirements

We assume you are totally new to programming. To make things easy for you, we use simple language throughout the book. And we simplify many of the technical terms into something more straight forward and human friendly. Most trade jargons are intentionally skipped.

This is an easy-read book that attempts to make concepts SIMPLE and STRAIGHTFORWARD. It does not aim to cover everything in App Inventor. It simply tries to get you started quickly.

You need to be computer literate. You should know how to use a web browser since App Inventor is web based. And you should have a reasonably configured computer system that comes with a dual core processor, 2GB+ of RAM, several GBs of free drive space that hold the resource files, and an active internet connection ... etc.

The MIT App Inventor is web based and can be accessed via: http://appinventor.mit.edu/explore/

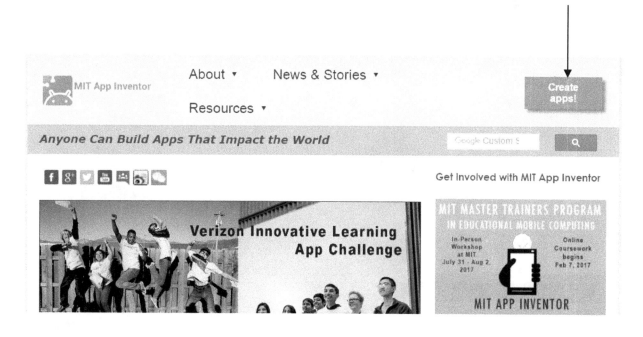

As of the time of this writing the latest version of App Inventor is nb 155 (App Inventor 2 beta).

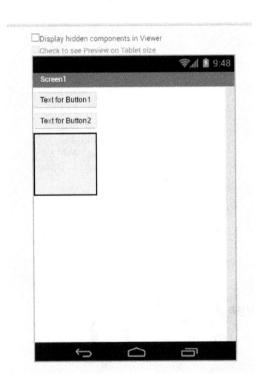

You need a proper web browser. The latest version of

Chrome is recommended. To be able to save your project,

you must first setup a Google email account and use it to

access App Inventor. A profile will be associated with this email.

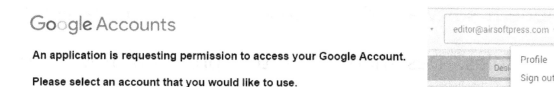

To get started you simply click Start New Project and then give the project a name.

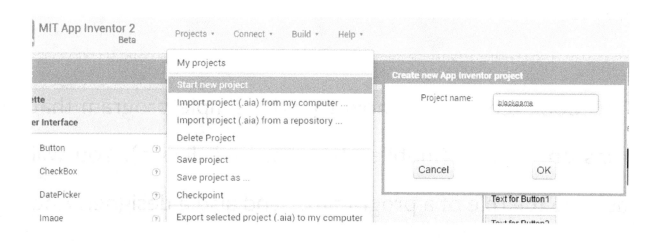

Learning Goals

In a modern software development venture there are 3 different roles. Designers plan the program flow and conceptualize the various program features. Artists draw the user interface elements and the surrounding environment so to create the look and feel of the program. Programmers implement the design accordingly by writing codes.

This book teaches you how to write simple program that runs on Android (mobile phone or pad device). You will assume the role of a programmer and also a designer. And you will learn to use ready-made artworks from opensource to speed up the software creation process.

The Target Platform

With the tools we introduce in this book it is actually possible to create programs that run on desktop computers (using Android emulator) and mobile devices (Android). The programs created by App Inventor can run on these platforms flawlessly. Keep in mind, App Inventor by default assumes that your project is to be run on mobile phone. The default screen layout is therefore based on that of a mobile phone.

Tools and Resources

We use the MIT App Inventor (Beta 2) to do the job. App Inventor is a drag and drop program design environment which also allows visual programming. Visual programming involves dragging "components". Simply put, you don't type codes - you drag and drop codes!

App Inventor is a general purpose app design environment extremely useful for learning purpose. It has 2 modes. The designer mode allows you to arrange the screen layout and components. The Blocks mode allows you to code visually.

Copyright 2017 **The HobbyPRESS (Hong Kong)**.

Lesson 1 - the concept of components and properties

Visual programming involves creating computer program using pictorial elements. App Inventor is special in that apart from drag and drop it also offers a block mode – you drag and drop code blocks to form a program.

The first thing we want you to know is that everything that gets shown on the design screen (the viewer) is a component (aka screen object). The Palette on the left accommodates all the available components. You pick and drag the desired components to the viewer to form a screen.

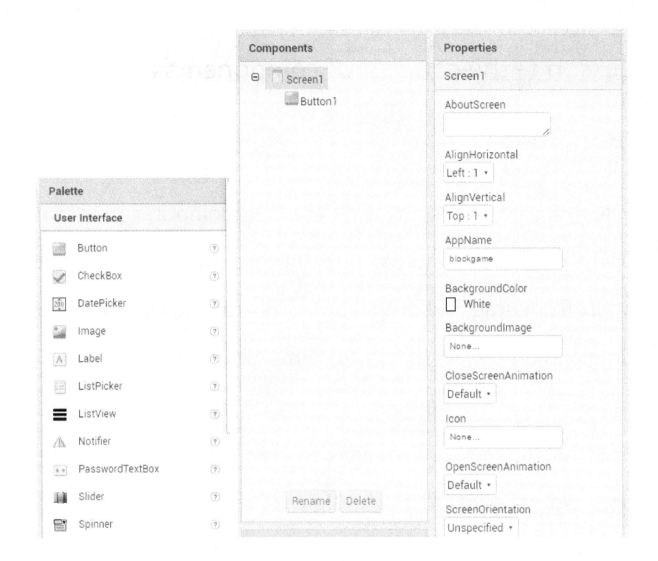

After placing the necessary components on the viewer, you define their basic behaviors through their properties.

For example, after placing an image component onto the viewer, you can specify the image content by setting its size and uploading a picture file for it:

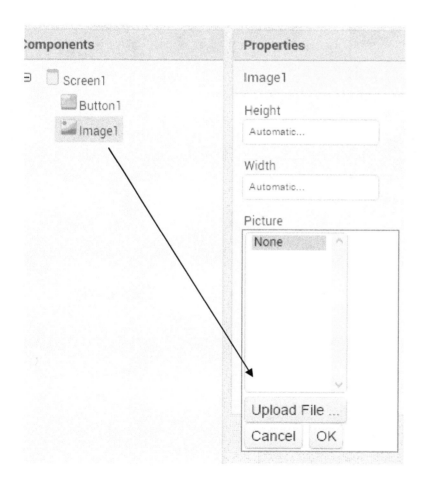

If the picture is too large, you can manually set its height and width. In other words, there is always room to fine tune the details.

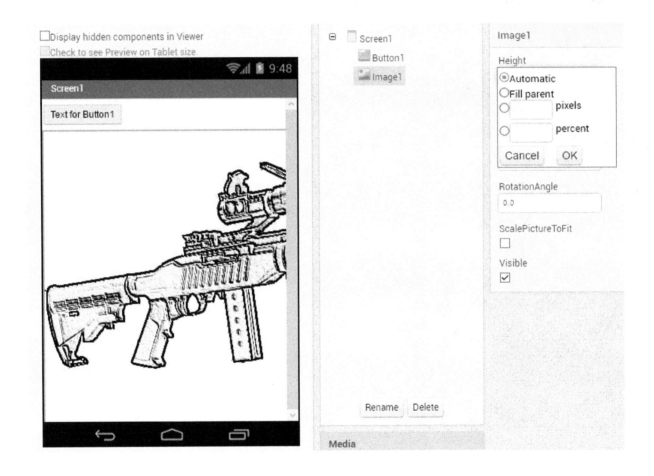

Lesson 1 con't – components interaction and

block programming

A program is all about interactions among component objects! In this short example, there is a button (called Click me) and an image.

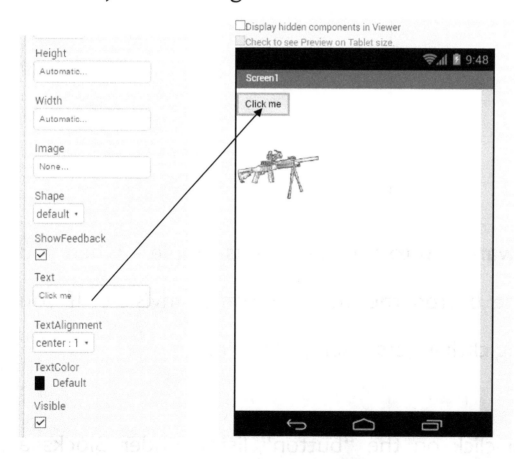

Copyright 2017 **The HobbyPRESS (Hong Kong)**.

Now switch to the block mode by clicking on Blocks.

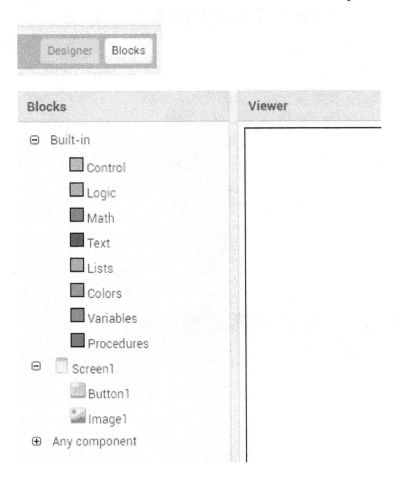

What we want you to achieve here is simple – when you click on the button the image becomes invisible. If you make a long click it gets displayed again.

When you click on the "button" listed under Blocks a

bunch of ready made code blocks are displayed automatically. Obviously you will find the first one and the third one useful.

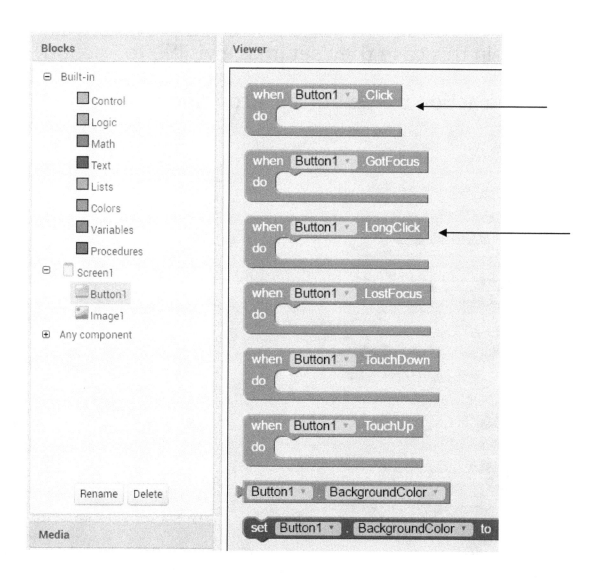

Lesson 1 con't – manipulating code blocks

First let's focus on the Click condition. You click to come up with a set of actions related to the image. Then pick the desired one (in this case the "set image visible to" action). Then drag the action to the button's condition.

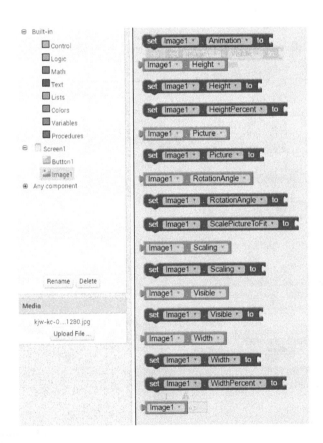

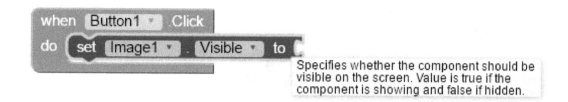

Specifies whether the component should be visible on the screen. Value is true if the component is showing and false if hidden.

Now you need to turn "visible" to "invisible". In other words, "visible" should be set to FALSE. Refer to the Logic section, you should drag False to the action.

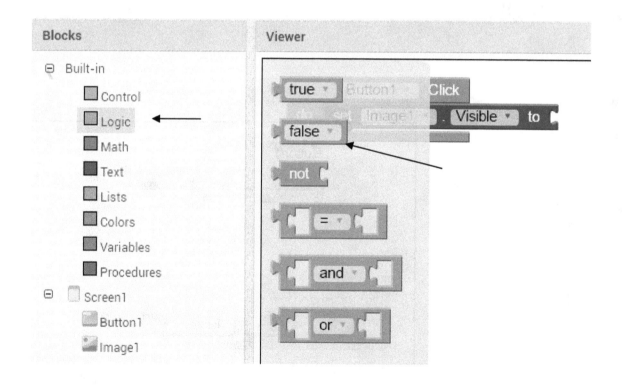

This is how the resulting block looks like:

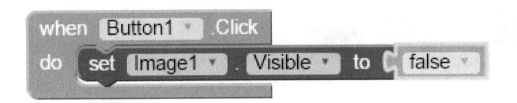

To define the second condition, click on the button again and pick another condition. Then click on the image to put together another action. This time you want to set visible back to TRUE.

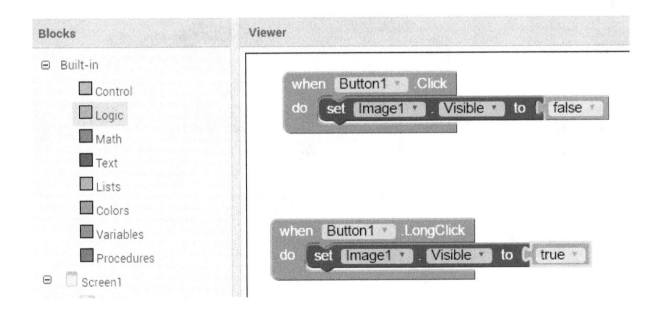

Lesson 1 con't – building and testing

To test the program on your mobile phone, first choose Build – App (provide QR code). App Inventor will compile the program into an APK file and give you a download link in the form of a QR code. Use any QR code reader on your mobile phone to read it and play the file accordingly.

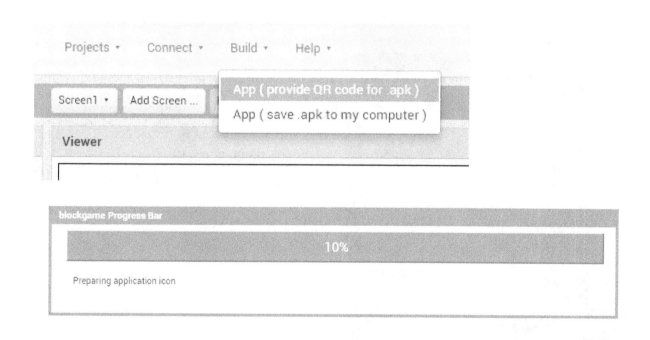

Barcode link for blockgame

OK

Note: this barcode is only valid for 2 hours. See the FAQ for info on how to share your app with others.

> Your mobile phone needs to have a QR Code reader in order to read it.

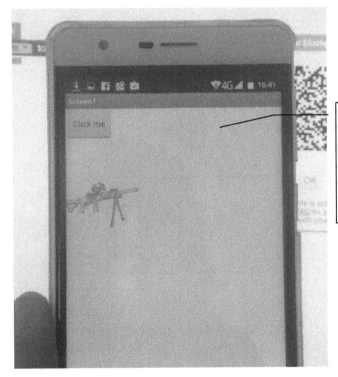

> The download link allows you to download an APK file. Once downloaded, the file needs to be installed in order to be played.

Copyright   2017

Lesson 1 con't - importing artworks

Artworks in a program are images that may be obtained from third parties free of charge (public domain artworks) or at a cost (or you may produce them from scratch). To use third parties images you need to first import them. You drag an image onto the viewer, then from the properties you click Picture and choose Upload file. This will allow you to import a third party image file for representing the current image component.

Major image formats such as JPG and BMP are supported.

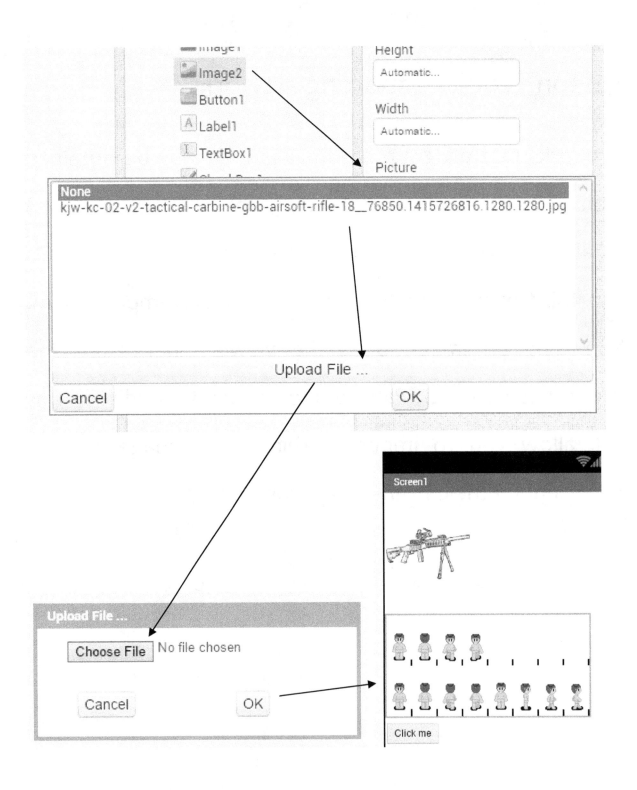

Lesson 1 con't - scaling imported artworks

If all you need is to set the scale of an image, you do not need to edit the original artwork. You simply set scaling. There are two actions for this purpose, one for the height and another for the width:

You need to assign a math value to each of these actions. Click on Math and choose the first one, plug it in to the actions and type in the proper values.

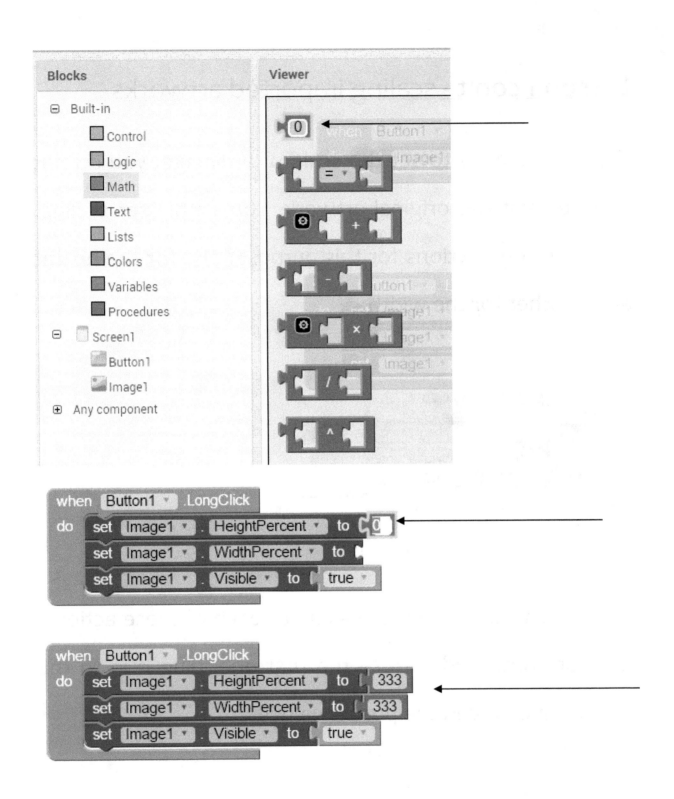

Copyright 2017 **The HobbyPRESS (Hong Kong)**. All rights reserved.

Oops ... there is an error which is not known until the program is run. It says the percentages must not be over 100...

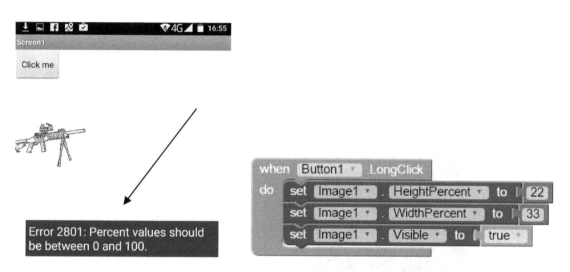

Error 2801: Percent values should be between 0 and 100.

That means, with the percentage settings you can hardly enlarge an image freely (the percentage is often relative to the screen so it requires careful trials to achieve the expected result). Fortunately, you can modify the action by changing to Height and Width respectively (so you can use any numeric values you like – the numeric values represent pixels). And as you can see, it is possible to modify an existing action pretty easily.

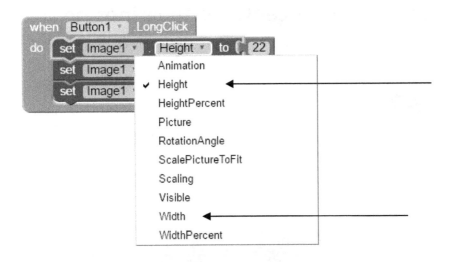

Lesson 2 – if then else logic

You can start to write a code block independently. See this example, the block starts with an IF logic which is from the Control section.

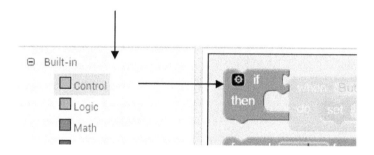

Let's say, if the image is visible, you want the button to stay green. But if the image is gone, you want the button to turn red. You need a control logic like this one:

You then need to manipulate the button's background

color and pick a color for it:

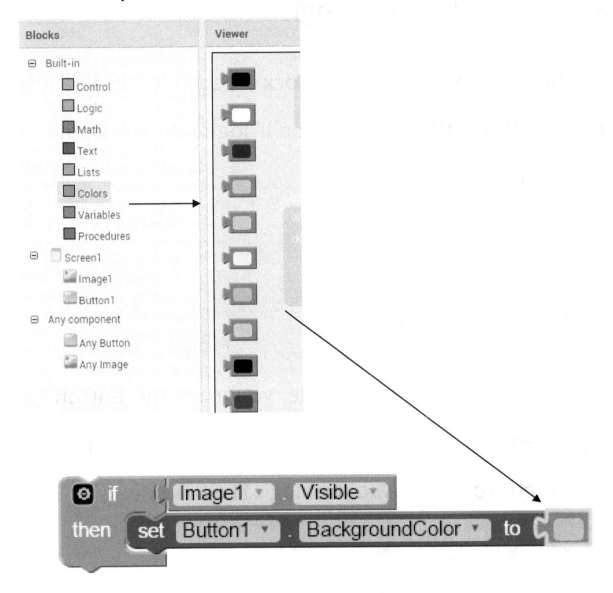

The green logic is done. How about the red? You can make

a separate block for the red, or change this to an IF THEN

ELSE block by dragging the ELSE to the IF.

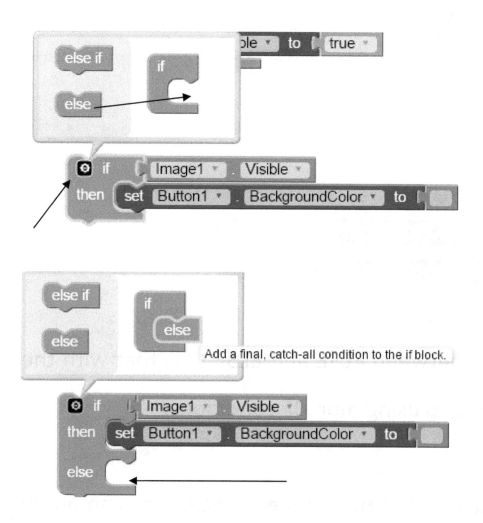

Now you can right click and choose to duplicate the background color action and place it under ELSE, then set the color to red.

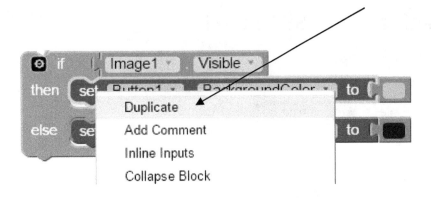

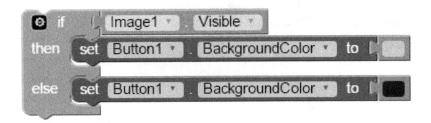

The difference between ELSE and ELSE IF is that with the latter you can keep using more IF conditions.

Note that within each THEN and each ELSE you can put in multiple actions:

Copyright 2017 **The HobbyPRESS (Hong Kong)**.

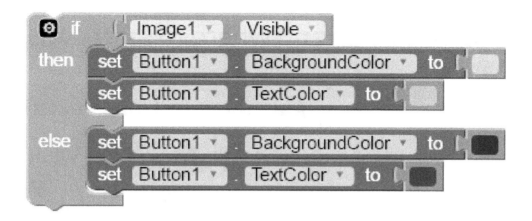

In theory you can put in as many actions as you like. If a block is not suitable, when you try to plug it in it will come back out immediately. Most of the time App Inventor knows what work and what does not.

Lesson 2 con't – when and where to start

Now when you run the program, you will find that the color changes do not take effect at all. To find out what is wrong, click on the warning sign and you will see a message like this:

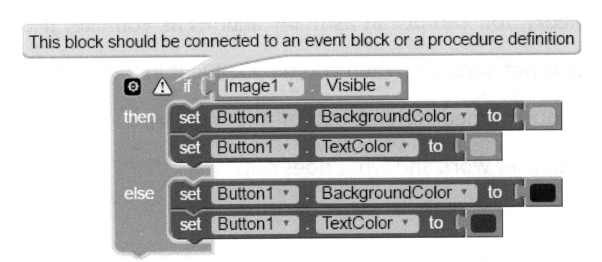

It seems like this block does not know when and where to start. Think about it – you want this color scheme to take effect when the program starts. So what you should do is to tell this block to run whenever the screen initializes.

Copyright 2017 **The HobbyPRESS (Hong Kong)**.

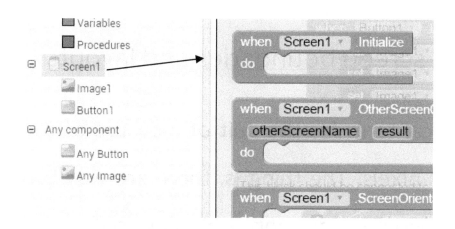

You can now plug the IF THEN ELSE code block into this Initialize condition and see how it goes.

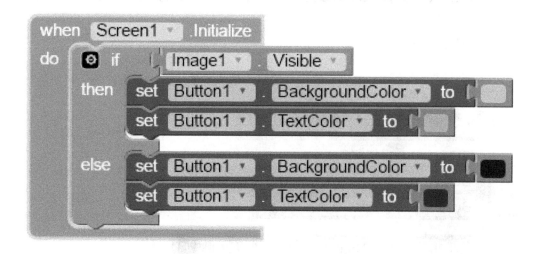

Lesson 2 con't - screen boundaries and layouts

The precise technical term for the unit of measure of the screen play area is pixels. The thing is, there are way too many different screen sizes on mobile phones so it would be difficult to set a proper size…. If in case what you have is too large for the phone display, setting the screen to scrollable may be helpful (user can scroll with one finger). You can simply add one action to the code block to make the screen scrollable:

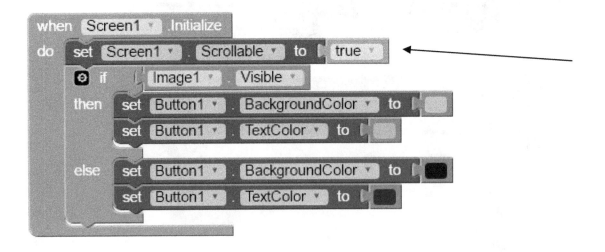

Copyright 2017 **The HobbyPRESS (Hong Kong)**.

If necessary you can change the screen orientation as well.

The screen orientation has to be a text value. "landscape", "portrait" and "sensor" are the more popular options. It is recommended that you try them out one by one on your phone.

"Sensor" means the orientation can change by rotating your phone.

Lesson 3 - accepting and processing user input

Different platforms accept different inputs. A mobile phone based program primarily takes input in the form of touch (touch up or touch down), focus (got or lost focus) and click (regular click or long click). You tie an input to a particular component (such as a button or a checkbox), and the other on screen components will take actions programmatically in response. As previously said, it is all about component interaction. That is, things that happen to one will cause some others to act and react. When you touch or click an on screen component that component will receive an event and trigger actions on itself and on others.

App Inventor provides predefined user input types for the available input objects. So all you need to do is to pick and use whatever is suitable for your code:

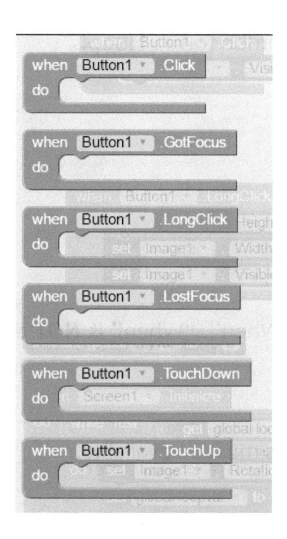

Lesson 3 con't - loop

A very important control logic you need to know is loop. A loop basically repeats things until a particular condition is met. A While loop is the most common form of loop.

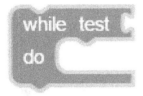

Do NOT confuse "While" with "When". "When" is NOT a loop!

For a loop to work, some variables must be available.

Lesson 3 con't – variables

A variable is a value that can change depending on the conditions encountered. App Inventor allows you to create variables that are not visible – in other words, they are not components that are displayed on screen but just "something" behind the scene. Under Variables there is a block called Initialize Global Name to ...

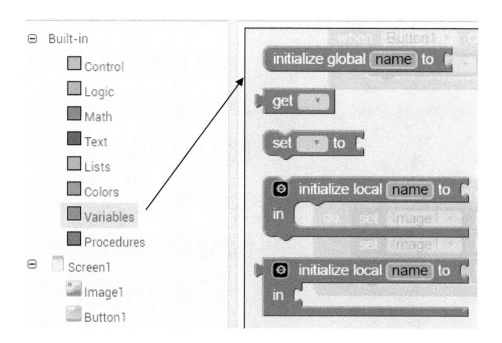

Global is the nature of the variable. It is global to the program, that means it can be used anywhere in the program. name is the variable name – you can type in any name you like to label the variable. Initialize a variable means you set up this variable and give it an initial value. From the Math section you pick a block and type in a numeric value for it.

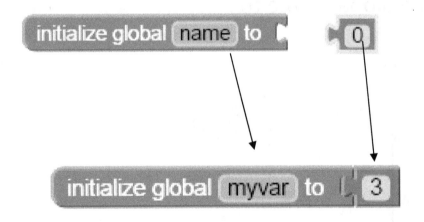

To later reference this variable, use Get:

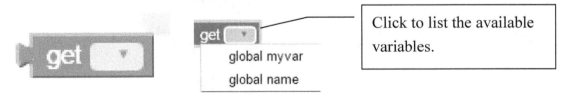

Click to list the available variables.

Say you want to set the button text to the value of the variable you have just defined, you can use this block:

For the thing to work, first you create and initialize the variable myvar to 3, then you set the button text to the value of myvar (which is 3 for now):

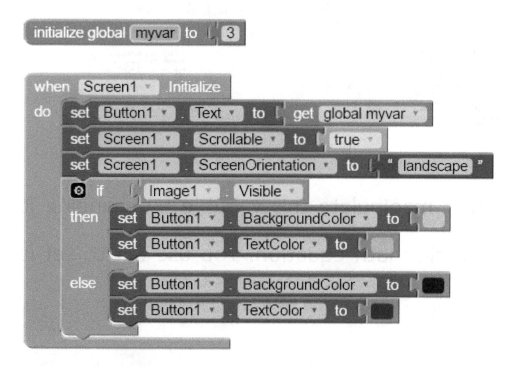

Copyright 2017

You must remember that a variable is not visible on screen. To display its value, you must refer to it from a screen component!

Not all components can accommodate such value. Generally, any variable with a Text property can take this value.

```
when  Screen1   .Initialize
do    set  Button1   .  Text   to    get  global myvar
      set  Label1    .  Text   to    get  global myvar
      set  TextBox1  .  Text   to    get  global myvar
      set  CheckBox1 .  Text   to    get  global myvar
```

You can further manipulate this variable by changing its value using simple math equation. You use Set to set its value:

You want to set its value to one which is the existing value times 12. So you use this math block:

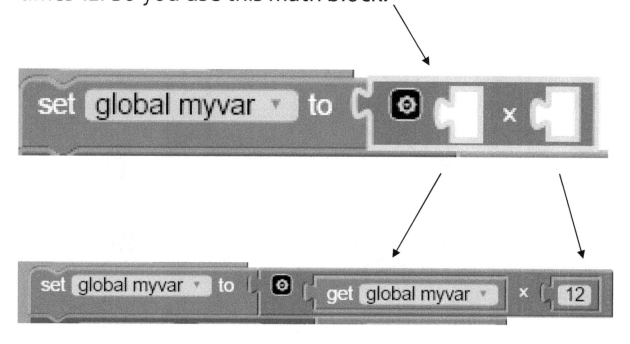

Now the whole block should look like this:

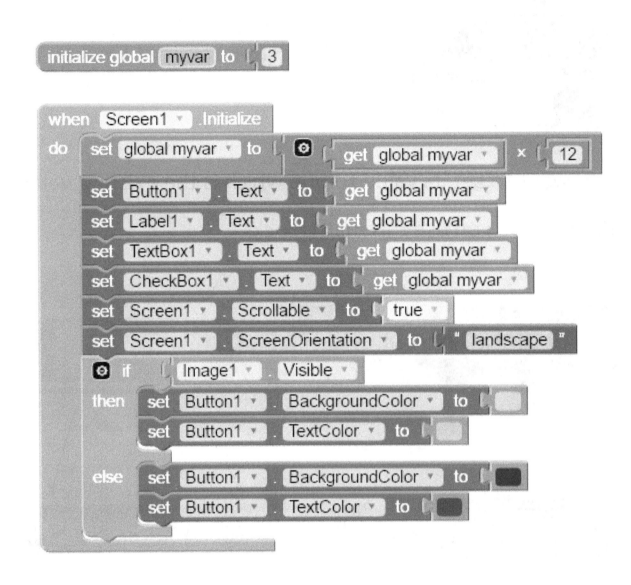

And this is how the result looks like:

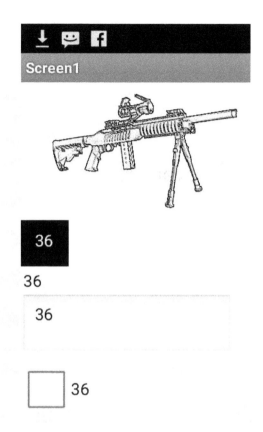

Note that a variable can be local or global. A local one is limited (i.e. local) to a block while a global one can work anywhere in the entire program. For simplicity sake only global variables are used in our demos.

Lesson 3 con't – revisiting loop

For a loop to work a variable is required. You need to create a new loop variable (named loopvar - it can be any name you like) and initialize it.

initialize global loopvar to 1

Now you set a while loop. This while loop needs a test condition. To construct a test condition, you need to use a comparison block from Logic.

You want the loop to continue as long as the value of loopvar does not reach 20 (or anything else).

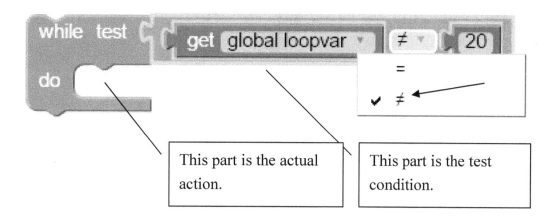

This part is the actual action.

This part is the test condition.

The action to take is to rotate the image. You set the image's rotation angle to the value of the loop variable. Then you increment the loop variable by 1 and let the loop goes on. The loop will keep repeating itself until the value of the loop variable reaches 20.

Now you need to plug the block into the code.

```
initialize global [ myvar ] to [ 3 ]
initialize global [ loopvar ] to [ 1 ]
when [ Screen1 ▼ ] .Initialize
do   while  test [ get [ global loopvar ▼ ] ≠ ▼ [ 20 ]
         do   set [ Image1 ▼ ] . [ RotationAngle ▼ ] to [ get [ global loopvar ▼ ]
              set [ global loopvar ▼ ] to [ ⊙ [ get [ global loopvar ▼ ] + [ 1 ]

     set [ global myvar ▼ ] to [ ⊙ [ get [ global myvar ▼ ] × [ 12 ]
     set [ Button1 ▼ ] . [ Text ▼ ] to [ get [ global myvar ▼ ]
     set [ Label1 ▼ ] . [ Text ▼ ] to [ get [ global myvar ▼ ]
     set [ TextBox1 ▼ ] . [ Text ▼ ] to [ get [ global myvar ▼ ]
     set [ CheckBox1 ▼ ] . [ Text ▼ ] to [ get [ global myvar ▼ ]
```

You can even change 20 to a random number. First you right click on 20and choose Delete block (this is how you delete and/or replace a block).

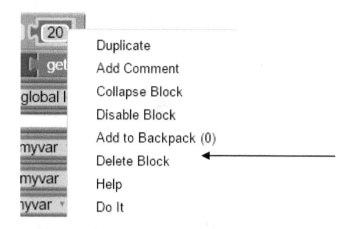

Then you go to Math and pick the Random integer block.

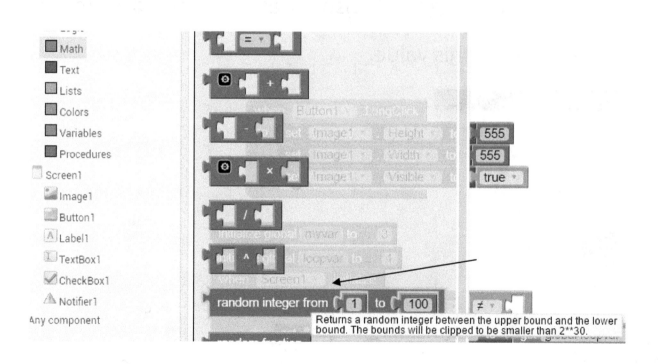

You plug this block in and give it a new range of values:

Now the loop will repeat for a different number of times based solely on the random value generated by App Inventor. The image will also rotate towards a different angle based on this value.

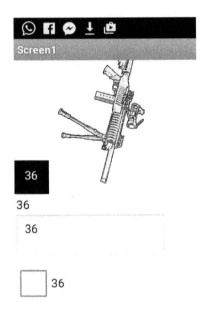

Lesson 3 con't - revisiting component interactions

You can set one component to influence another, or to react to actions of another. You do this through using a When Do block. With a When Do block, whatever happens to one component can be used to trigger actions on the others. For example, the follow block says when the screen initializes, the other items will set their text...

You can change it to, say, whenever the button receives

focus, the other components will set their text accordingly... To replace the existing when condition, you pull out the code block held within it, then get a new when block and plug back in...

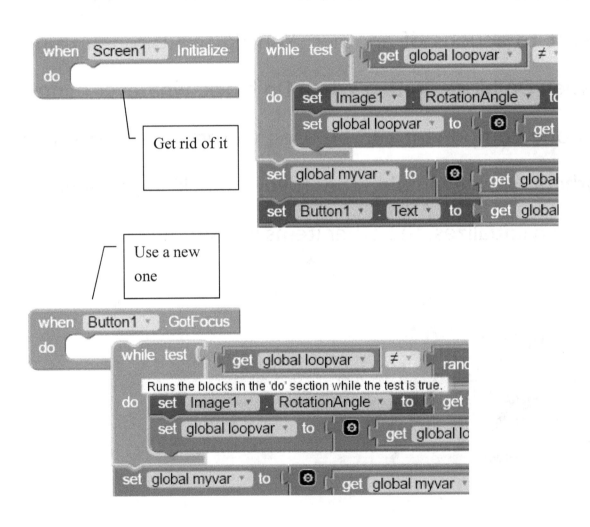

Copyright 2017 **The HobbyPRESS (Hong Kong).** All rights reserved.

You may not use multiple when conditions together. These when blocks simply won't fit with each others.

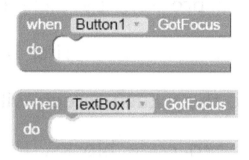

There are some complicated ways to use multiple when conditions, but they are out of the scope of this starter book.

Lesson 4 – dealing with multiple screens

You can add another screen to the program by clicking Add Screen (but Screen1 will always get opened first by default - there is no way to change this). Each screen will have its own set of components and code blocks. The Button1 on screen2 is not the same as the Button1 on screen1.

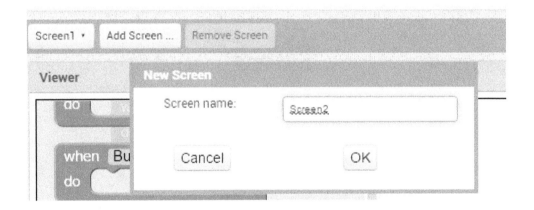

There are actions for manipulating screens. For example,

by pressing the button of screen2 you can call up screen1:

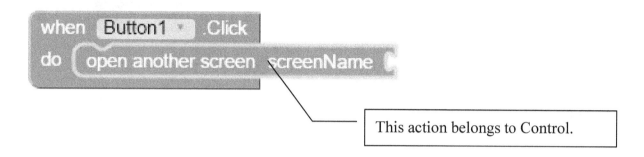

This action belongs to Control.

You need to tell which screen to open. The screen name should be supplied as text. Do remember, the screen name is always case sensitive! If you specify the wrong name you will receive a runtime error!

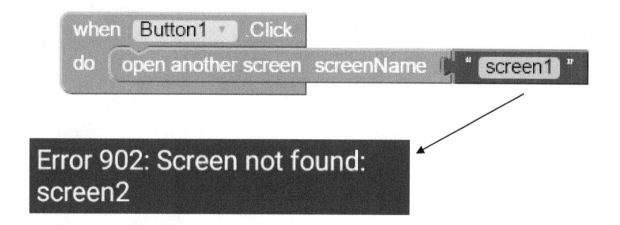

Error 902: Screen not found: screen2

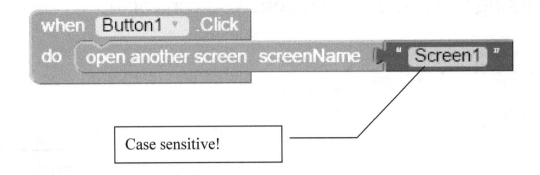

Case sensitive!

When you call up another screen (say, Screen2) and later you want to go back to the previous screen (Screen1), instead of opening Screen1 you should just close Screen2. Screen1 wasn't closed at all when you opened up Screen2 from there. So, by closing Screen2 you will see Screen1 again.

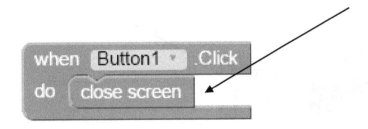

Lesson 4 con't – closing the program

To allow your user to close the program, you should have a button capable of closing the program. The action to use is close application, which is capable of shutting down the entire program (and all its screens).

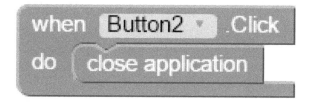

END OF BOOK

Please email your questions and comments to admin@Tomorrowskills.com.

Copyright 2017 **The HobbyPRESS (Hong Kong)**.

www.ingramcontent.com/pod-product-compliance
Lightning Source LLC
Chambersburg PA
CBHW061628080326
40690CB00058B/4285